Journey in the Mind's Eye of a Poet: A Search for Faith

BOOK FOUR (2009 TO 2010)

Moods of War

Conflicts in Faith

Tony Prewit

Journey in the Mind's Eye of a Poet: A Search for Faith
Book Four (2008 to 2009): Moods of War

copyright Tony Prewit, 2012

Published by Ridgeline Press
Silver City, New Mexico, U.S.A.
ISBN 978-0-9854487-3-8

Editing, book design, cover design, and production services by
Heidi Connolly, Harvard Girl Word Services
Cover artwork by Tony Prewit

Acknowledgments

I would like to thank my wife, Patricia Prewit, for the years of assistance in sorting, editing, and proofreading all my work. I thank her most of all for her being her and allowing me to continue to be the person she married. I would also like to thank Sarah Johnson, a professional proofreader, who offered intelligent suggestions in shaping these books and gave me a valuable critique of its quality and content. Finally, I would like to thank the friends who read the complete series, contributed valuable suggestions, and urged me to arrange it into the form it has become: Gretchen Van Auken, Charlie Mckee, and Gail Rein. I thank Raymond Hornbaker for the years of commitment to our late-night discussions. I would also like to mention the editor who helped with the final sculpture of these books, Heidi Connolly, whose vision, talent, and professional guidance have been invaluable.

Table of Contents

Prologue   vii

Part One: The War Journal   13

Excerpts (1 to 14)   15
In Conclusion   37
Story of the Old Meadow War   38
The Old Meadow War Song   55

Part Two: Moods of War Rhapsody   57

Rhapsody: Moods of War (1)   59
Rhapsody: Moods of War (2)   63
Rhapsody: One Woman Said   67
Rhapsody: Kings of War   68

Part Three: The Tunnel Dreams   75

Tunnel Dreams (1 to 4)   77
A Dream of the Mercy of God   91
Epilogue   94
The Night After   95
No Rest Here   96
The Warrior Gods   97
It Is No Crime   99

Part Four: Place of Lights   101

We All Go to Heaven   103
Place of Lights   104
It Is a Place   105
Place of Lights 1 to 3   106

Awareness   108
I Am Without Shame   109
Thoughts About God   110

Part Five: Dream Chronicles (1974-1977)   111

    The Room of My Father   113
    Brick and Steel Are One   114
    Of Pearls and Men   117
    It Just Was   118
    Bread and Butter and a Bomb   119
    Where Brick and Steel Cringe   120
    A New Adam and Eve (1 to 5)   122
    Last Testament   131
    Utopia Bazaar   132

Prologue

These six books are written in a poetry/prose form, a process that spans thirty-five years and encompasses the gradual evolution into my inner search for a personal faith and belief in God. It is a poet's journal and also like a novel in poetry form, one in which I am the narrator as well as a main character. The poems document my gradual disengagement with traditional, conservative, evangelical Christianity as I built a belief and faith of my own. Although I certainly did not have this defined purpose when I started this journal, it matured this way over time to become collection of six books that record a journey in search of a faith I could call my own.

As I walk away from the Christianity in which I once believed without doubting the existence of a God, I continue to discover a place within where I am learning how to build my own faith. This writing is for those who are at a dead end or a crossroad in their belief, or in a dysfunctional relationship (so to speak) with their spiritual beliefs. One of my messages, therefore, is that our spiritual beliefs do not have to be unchangeable.

Consequently, these poems are not so much a criticism of Christianity as they are a process of learning to ask the right questions. Over time I have learned to be wary of those who do not want to hear my questions and who are defensive toward honest doubt and inquiry. Because I was trapped in a doctrine that did not allow me to express my belief in my own way, and because I wanted to keep my Christian friends, I kept silent for many years.

The poems in this work capture my observations and reflections about how I see life through the veil of my own struggle, and will hopefully allow others to consider the shortcomings of their own beliefs, or of any belief that does not allow for true dialog. Because none of us really knows the truth for sure when it comes to belief, it would appear that there are shortcomings in all spiritual belief systems, regardless of form. For that reason, we are left to ourselves to construct a satisfactory — and satisfying — faith.

The stunning effect of this pursuit is my finding that God gets larger from the inside out. This is where my journey has found its pleasure and its peace, even while admitting the sorrow and fear of the search.

I have wrestled with my soul along this path and it wrestled back, for what I was struggling with was my spiritual identity. In wrestling, I learned the value of putting forth the right questions rather than assuming I had the right answers.

In fact, questions have become answers in their own right for me, for a light turned on in the asking that helped illuminate my way. I further learned that without questions we have no way to really appreciate where we are going and why. As such, I am thankful that I realized the importance of questions within the arena of spiritual beliefs.

The six books in this series are (in order): *Journal of Time*, *Portals and Passages*, *The Book of the Lost and Found* or *Chasing Rainbows*, *Moods of War*, *The Source*, and *Another Day*.

Book One is the beginning of my realizations and observations of life, which I describe as "me looking inside me from the perspective of the outside me," and then, "me looking outside me from the perspective of the inside me." It is the discovery of my need for a faith in God of my own. Book Two is a confession of my dreams and the effect dreams can have upon one's life. Book Two also reveals my earliest thoughts concerning my spiritual beliefs, kept very secret until then, and how these secrets became a burden to my search for faith. In Books Three and Four I begin to focus my writing toward a more intense spiritual inquiry based on my discontentment with religious answers. These two works became like a great mountain I needed to climb, blocking the path of what I considered my "true" journey. One might also describe them as an inner wrestling match where the rule was to fight to the finish. In total these books are the recording of how I lost my past faith and discovered what I call "conflicts of faith." Hence, Book Five is the result of feeling as if I had reached the top of the mountain, had a good view of a long way down the road, and could tell that although the journey was long from over, I was sensing a peace that came from finding my own faith. Book Six is about learning to live with the faith I had created.

Phrases and Words

The phrase "Treat others as we want them to treat us" is the most frequently used phrase in these books, and it has become more important to me as the years have passed. It has become a part of the foundation of my own faith because no matter how I might try, it stuck with me, withstanding all inquiry, doubt, and question.

To treat others as we want them to treat us simply means to me that we value others as equal to ourselves and value their needs as important as our own. And that if we do not wish to be cheated, lied to, deceived, oppressed, or manipulated, then we should be willing not to cheat, lie, deceive, oppress, or manipulate others.

I use other Judeo-Christian terms such as "heaven" and "hell" and the duality of "good" and "evil." These terms and their meanings come from my own culture and western traditional Christian teaching. I do not necessarily consider these terms to be universally accepted as truth; they serve only as my own points of reference into my inner spiritual search.

My use of the word "God" in the masculine form is habit and based somewhat on the limitations of the English language. In my mind, God is of no gender, no religion, no race, no culture.

In some parts you may find the writing in these books somewhat redundant. The repetitiveness serves as an accurate picture of my perspective, however, for I believe we are all in the process of being formed and we repeat our thoughts and feelings until they either become a part of us or fade.

My style of writing is varied. It weaves poetry, commentary, and prose. I do not attempt to stay inside the lines of strict grammatical compliance. I give myself poetic license. I am much more concerned with content and the work's original form than with adherence to rules. You'll see I have also invented a few words along the way.

Initially, my poetry/journal was not produced as a neat stack of notebooks; instead, scattered notebooks, legal pads, single sheets, and scratch paper filled with writings piled up until the notebooks piled up on top of each other. They were in no real order. No, I did not have a neat stack at all. In fact, after thirty-five years' worth of notebooks had turned into a kind of organizational nightmare, I felt it was almost futile to even attempt to sort through it all. Common sense prevailed, however, and this six-book format is the result of sorting and compiling a presentable record of my writings.

Part One:
The War Journal

Excerpt 1

why the "moods of war" are in my soul
i scarcely know
    though i know they are strong
    within me
        — why?

what kind of God has designed us this way
    where the thought of war
    is like a virtue and a righteousness
        and a defense of God
            — why?

is this conflict that resides in us
the will of God
    because we gravitate
        toward it so naturally
            — why?

it is as if we are waiting for a reason to war
as if it holds the promise that war of any kind
    will bring us closer to God

what is this in us that entertains such thoughts
    — and why?

if the moods of war are in us
and if they are from God
    then there must be a right and good use of them.

Excerpt 2

herein lies the problem:
 believing that God has ordained us to convert
  and rule the world
   means only that others believe the same

 can we lay down the weapons
 that cause this evil mood of war to rise up in us
  as an aggression against any who believe in God
  in a different way?

these weapons of belief are in the form of a
 "one and only true way to God"
the belief that God has ordained and commanded us
 to convert the world to this way of thinking
these weapons are the most dangerous
 dividing friends families neighbors churches
 nations governments and religions

though we are on a war path we see it as a virtue
 and as the work of God
 the puzzle is why we gravitate to these
 weapons so naturally.

Excerpt 3

How much do we have to see before we see the insanity?

Is all we want to be in God's will, the desire strong within us?

Can we find the will of God without the belief that there has to be a one and only true way to God and that we have to force the world to that belief?

Are there not many ways to God, and can we not honor them all? What is it that God wants for us? Why does He wait so patiently for us to discover Him? Would it not be easier if God made His wishes known to us? Why does He offer so little assistance to us in this pursuit?

Herein lies the most startling question of all, then: Why is God so silent? And why do we place such eternal consequences on knowing the "truths" about which He remains so mum? The humility of this reality, that none of us knows for sure what is spiritually true and that we all approach God through faith, must be based on the fact that God's silence must be the determining factor for how we define faith.

Perhaps the key is that God wants us to know that it is by faith we conceive of the reality of an unseen God without God's revealing it any other way. And if God, through silence, shows me this truth then I am humbled by the fact that none of us really knows for sure what is spiritually true, yet can still conceive of the reality of an unseen God. Therefore, is it that God wants us to seek for Him and be humbled by His silence?

Knowing that God chooses to keep silent and that none of us knows for certain what is true in this spiritual realm, why do we insist that we know the "real" spiritual truths — that there is one and only true way to God and that *our* way is that one and only true way to God? And why are we willing to risk so much on our knowing?

> *the evidence of our ignorance speaks loudly*
> *the knowledge of God remains silent*
> *defending is in our nature*
> *and leads us to cruelties*
> *unconcerned about the moods of war within*
>
> *is there a reason for its existence*
> *— for its arousal?*
> *if so let us beware of how it causes us to behave cruelly and*
> *with intent to harm*
> *is now not the time for reexamination?*
>
> *i see the moods of war as real*
> *i see God as mostly silent*
> *— two truths that unnerve me enough that I am not*
> *satisfied to continue down the same path of religious belief*
> *to insist on one and only true way to God*
>
> *for the silence of God is humbling*
> *and none of us is without blame*
> *justified in our assertion that we have*
> *the one and only true way to God*

can we not lay down these weapons of cruelty and justification?

Excerpt 4

My questions start like this: Does any religion that seeks to remove our freedom of choice also take our will to seek God in the way He intended?

If my freedom of choice to believe in God is deep within me, then there are thieves out to steal it from me in the name of God. The men who stand in the pulpits want us as puppets, giving us only enough freedom to believe as they want or be threatened by the lack of a pulpit, an authority without value. And without the value of power and authority, what would they have?

Within the freedom of choice a duality of good and evil exists, and in that duality lies our struggle, the struggle of belief.

I say I have the right to defend my belief to anyone and that the moods of war that rise up in me are justified as a defense against those who would condemn my belief.

I extend this right to all people: to defend their belief when challenged, to believe in God as they choose, to defend against any who challenges this right.

> *my God, humble me*
> *to respect all people*
> *to not raise a weapon*
> *in the name of a belief in*
> *one and only true way to God*

If God desires us to give each other the room and freedom to believe in God as we will, then condemnation of another's belief could very well mean we are fighting against God.

I seek to do no harm even in defense of my spiritual beliefs; however, if I am attacked, I have the right to defend myself. And if my defense harms my attacker then know there is a difference between one who defends and one who attacks.

I believe in a God by faith, and though I am unsure of my truth concerning God, it suits me, and I know my belief is no better than yours. I believe we are equal in this way, and if we could all see ourselves as equal then we would have no need for the moods of war within us to be aroused. If we stop challenging spiritual beliefs, perhaps real peace and respect could then exist amongst us. But this is not yet the case, so I must explore further the moods of war.

Excerpt 5

1.

if the moods of war are in us
then i ask You God
show me how to use them
for if left up to my own devices
i will surely stumble

As my prayer began to fade, my thoughts suddenly
saw a "construction zone" in the road of my journey,
which then took a detour. It was at that point my thoughts
said to me, "Do not turn away from this detour, but take it
and see where it leads."

I can now say that this detour caused me to look
further inside, for as I passed the construction zone I
could see how much the road was in need of repair.
Diverging in this way helped me discover a part of me I
had never known before, a place where I could find the
innate common knowledge that is in us all . . . a place
where perhaps the real word of God existed as well.
Was it possible that we could identify a common base of
knowledge in all our written bibles and sacred writings
and that we could agree on common understandings? I
believe so.

I also ask: if we all instinctively react to defend
our beliefs against any who would seek to undermine,
condemn, or destroy them because of *their* innate need to
defend *their* belief in God, does that mean God honors all
beliefs as equal?

It was in discovering this place of "innate common
knowledge" that I heard God speak into His silence by
way of what He has written in us at birth.

So, is there evidence of God's word in what is innately common in us all?

2.

This next thought came quickly, invading the thought I'd just recorded: How is it that we have so many versions of the truth, and why do the believers of these different versions have to insist that their version is the right one?

Could it be that God provides all people of different cultures, experiences, circumstances, and time the revelations and truths that will guide them? Or is it more likely that these revelations are specific to specific cultures, experiences, circumstances, and times . . . and are not necessarily universal truths for everyone?

If our bibles and sacred writings reveal such revelations, then it requires some humility to see that there could be many bibles and sacred writings for that reason. But then why would God write so many different versions and theologies and then give them to us to form all these different religions, groups, cultures, and subgroups within the same religions?

Why would God write so many versions of the truth that we have so much conflict amongst us . . . and then tell each group that its particular way of approaching God is the one and only true way to reach Him?

Could it be that in fact there is no written word of God on tablets or pages, but rather that He has already written His word upon us before birth . . . and that His word is identified by what is innately common in us all? In that case, we would have no need of a written word to find Him.

It is when we insist our interpretation is the right interpretation and our book is the right book that we become ripe

*for divisions, conflicts, prejudices, intolerance, bigotry, and war. . .
and that does not sound like God to me.*

And what about the testimonies of missionaries
who say they offer their lives in sacrifice out of love and
concern for those who do not believe as they do? How is
it that this "love" gradually shifts, to be woven into the
tapestry of enforcement by the belief that those who do not
believe as they do will be condemned by God eternally?

Is such intolerance madness . . . cruelty . . . both?

Excerpt 6

More questions . . .

Is the reason we gravitate to the moods of war evidence that God has written it in us to do so? . . . And if the duality of good and evil is in us, has God written that in us as well? If so, then perhaps we need to wonder who is to blame for the evil in us.

If our religions and beliefs in God cause us to be in conflict with each other, then they are also the cause of many wars around the world. If God does speak differently to different peoples, how does God explain the fact that these differences cause so much war amongst us?

Why would God play cat-and-mouse or hide-and-seek games with the truth of life and put our lives at stake in the process? For we are a people that use the moods of war quickly, attacking others in justification of our spiritual beliefs in the most cruel and ungodly ways.

Does God in His tolerance allow us many different beliefs and approaches to Him?

Is it our intolerance that causes us to war with each other over these differences? If so, why is He so silent on this matter?

It appears that the duality of our good and evil is an obvious flaw; does God hold Himself to blame for this flaw?

Excerpt 7

1.

Have we been created in a way that is supposed
to test our faith, our choices, and our ability to come to
terms with the duality of this good and evil within us? If
so, why? What need would God have to test us? If we are
flawed with imperfections at birth, and our duality is the
primary imperfection, then we will certainly fail the test.

You are our Creator and we are the created.

You hold the future of the afterlife in Your hand.

Have we been created to face an eternal reward or
punishment? Are we to be condemned to Hell or rewarded
with Heaven based upon how we handle this duality?

I do not believe that You have created us for that
reason. I do believe the startling truth is that because of the
duality between good and evil that resides in us we need
protection from each other. Therefore, the idea of eternal
reward and punishment is only in our imagination. Yes, I
dare to say that the idea is ours, not God's.

Does man need the idea of reward and punishment
for himself on the earth? I can see that God might allow us
to use punishment and reward as a way to rule ourselves
on the earth and as a way to regulate ourselves . . . for we
can be cruel, and if we do not police ourselves then we
have no future on earth.

If it is God's plan for us to ultimately exist in an
eternal realm called Heaven and Hell, I do not see it.
Rather I see that in our reach for God we imagine God's
realm to be like our own realm on earth.

2.

Does Your silence tell us that our fate is already determined and allow us to create our own laws?

If our fate after death is already determined then I believe all people go to heaven. And if we are allowed to create our own laws, it is to protect ourselves from the good and evil that are in us at birth. I believe that You do not hold us not liable for wrong choices, but perhaps in Your silence You are saying that our fate is already determined.

There are many people who claim God is not silent and speaks to them constantly, but it seems to me that if God were really talking to us that way our lives and our wisdom would be overflowing . . . and the world would not be in this condition.

> *therefore it seems we are mostly on our own here*
>
> *yet the reality of God is strong within us*
>
> *and we are really unsure*
>
> *of the relationship between us.*

3.

Reward and punishment are needed on the earth as a means of protection from each other. If we can learn to value other people's spiritual beliefs as equally important to them as our own are to us, and to treat others with honesty and respect, I believe we could undergo transformation, as could our work undergo transformation into a more peaceful place.

My journey is not complete and my reflections here are not complete either. I share them knowing they are still evolving as we all are.

Excerpt 8

1.

It is evening and I am watching the stars in the sky. Gradually I am taken in by the sight. To me it is like worship, and I bow at the wonder of it all. I imagine that many others watch the evening sky and are taken in by its beauty and are in awe as well.

A man named Abraham comes to mind, for in the Old Testament of the Bible Abraham gives testimony of how he came to a belief concerning his relationship to God and about how he also watched the evening skies.

If Abraham is correct in his concept of his relationship to God, then I am comforted. For he proclaimed that God considered him righteous because of his willingness to believe in an unseen God. This, to me, means that Abraham perceived in his heart, mind, and spirit that it was through the spirit that one reaches out to God, that it is through faith that the spirit performs that "reaching out," and that through spirit we perceive the reality of the unseen God. To Abraham, this was a righteous act, one that convinced him that he was considered a righteous man by God for reaching out to God in faith in this way.

Am I, then, also righteous because I reach out to God? If I have discovered that I reach out with my spirit in faith then have I discovered the meaning of righteousness, at least according to Abraham?

The evening sky engulfs my soul; I perceive I am in a spiritual place, and I am rested now because of it.

2.

When my spirit moves in faith this way, makes itself known to me, and makes known to me the unseen God, I perceive these words — inaudible, yet clearly heard:

you and i are of the same spirit
i am moved in the spirit by faith
i see where God dwells

a part of God dwells in me
and in you
and is with us always

God's voice in us is heard
through the fruits of the spirit
and these fruits are inside us.

Excerpt 9

Though God touches me not, am I guilty of imagining His touch? As I look inside further I see, to my horror, that it is only me touching me and imagining it to be God.

I am fooled by own voice which offers me solace and advice. I want it so much to be God's voice that I am fooled. So, where is God's voice, then?

As I examine this voice I see that God has given it to me, and to all of us, that we may speak to ourselves and comfort ourselves, and draw upon it for answers to our lives. And therein lies a sort of spiritual reservoir, one which God has placed in each of us.

Though God remains silent, He also has shared a part of Him so we can call on Him through the fruits of the spirit, even though it is the voice of our own spirit we hear that leads us there. Some people may call the fruits of the spirit by another name, but to me the intent is the same.

Excerpt 10

1.

If you disagree with me
then debate with me
you are a fool
For to disagree is not wrong
It is better we debate with a passion for truth
and still be able to be friends
rather than be friends based upon agreement only
Let our friendships be formed
on seeing each other as equal in value

Let us argue our beliefs as if we both do not know for sure
Let us argue not to be right but for a better truth
It would be good if our arguments did not interfere with
our friendship
and it would be even better if the arguments deepened
our friendship as well

God is greater than all theologies
God has no need of theologies
God allows us to imagine theologies
Perhaps God inspires these theologies

If these theologies teach us to live with one another
without the moods of war
then we will have certainly come a long way
If not then I believe God will wait

> *if we are truly known by the fruits of our walk*
> *then any approach to God that inspires us*
> *to treat others as we want to be treated*
> *is the real proof of our closeness to God.*

2.

It seems that God waits for us to discover
and to learn how to live peacefully upon the earth
till our time is up.

3.

All have equal access to God
God is truly tolerant of all His creation
No one is left out
Let us allow each other the room to approach Him
the way we choose

God is big enough to work with any belief
That which is innately common to us all
is where God is to be found.

Excerpt 11

I heard a voice speaking to me from inside myself with a new thought: "Bring me your offering and name it whatever you want. Build your sanctuaries and fill them with any items you want. Seek Me on any day you want and call it any name you want.

"I am not caged by one thought of Me, nor do I give man a single approach to Me. You must come on your own and offer up to Me what it is you are willing to believe. No one is turned away, and everyone will receive My mercy the same. Any who seeks Me, I consider the righteous of the earth.

"I have made you and you will return to Me after you die, for My error in creation has fallen on you, and the ultimate burden is Mine.

"There is no place called Hell . . . it does not exist . . . I have no need of it. . . .

"You are linked to the earth for as long as you exist, and your spirit returns to Me. Your imperfect parts will cease to exist."

what of this new thought . . . of God's mercy

what of this new thought – that my spirit returns to God

i know there is more

and i must continue on this journey to find it

Is it up to us to determine the nature of our laws and civilizations? Is it we who need rewards and punishments to defend and protect ourselves from one another?

If so, then Heaven and Hell is man's concept, and reward and punishment only an adjunct approach necessary from and for mankind on earth—not something God needs.

Should we interpret God's silence as giving us the room to believe what we want?

Is His silence approval?

Excerpt 12

The mystery of man is a mystery still; though I may discern how to be at peace here on earth, I may not ever know the mystery of why we are here or why others feel compelled to pit themselves against each other for no other reason than their differing beliefs about God.

There are people who carry the weapon of belief of the one and only true way to God, and carry it everywhere, as do their leaders. That is why the moods of war are so easily aroused and there is always war at our heels.

Pursuit of life's mysteries is permanently detoured, therefore, with too little time to contemplate a world without war, no matter which side we take.

How insane is that?

Excerpt 13

I believe there are no written words of God and no Messiahs that represent the one and only true way to God. I believe God is bigger than any religion or theology or messiah.

I do not think that Jesus or any other human who carries a similar message would want us to make them the focus of righteousness; rather, I think they would want their message to be our focus and for us to know that they are as we are . . . human.

To me, the real and true God shares the throne with no other. If we do not want to be lied to, then we should not lie to others. If we do not want to be oppressed, cheated, or deceived, then we should not oppress, cheat, or deceive others.

Excerpt 14

The ownership of an intimate and personal spiritual experience with God is not necessarily exclusive to any of us based upon our "right" beliefs.

Know that others can and do have the same kinds of spiritual experiences even though their form of worship or expression may differ from ours. Consider the possibility that their spiritual experiences with God are equal to ours.

In Conclusion

Here is my proposition: Lay down this weapon of the moods of war as an aggressive force against others.

Period.

The burden of the duality of good and evil is enough to keep us busy on earth without being burdened with eternal judgment after death based on a belief that there is only one right and true way to God.

Story of the Old Meadow War
Rural town, USA, in the days before automobiles

i search my soul
to find the place where we are friends again

i see in my soul a distant memory
when we were children
when we met at the old meadow
till the sun went down
the only rule fair play

how i long for that day
that rule again
now that we are grown
with all our needs and greed

we have learned new doctrines
new creeds to live by
the rule of fair play
now only child's play

who could have known that our soul
would crave that rule from the past
from our childhood days

there is some wisdom born to us
without need of a teacher

like children with friends
spending their afternoons in play
is it in the children that the real answer lies?

Once upon a time. . .

   As I often do, I climbed the top of the hill for a view of the village where I grew up, and where my parents and their parents grew up. I enjoy looking down on the village from this solitary place, where I can be alone and search my soul. It is my way of worshiping and listening for God. Usually the view from the top of this hill is peaceful, but today this was not true and what I saw happening below sent a chill through my heart.

   The village was stirring with grit, swirling dust from many horses' hooves causing confusion and fear. The noise of the hooves and the screams of the people echoed upward and my ears ached from the sound of despair. I saw people running out of a building ablaze with flames. I became outraged, then sad, for clearly the rumor had come to pass. I did not know exactly what had sparked this conflict into violence, but because I wanted to learn the details I hastened back down the hill.

   The conflict, between the two main religious factions of the village, had finally reached a pinnacle of cruelty in its willingness to debase and instill fear.

   What had caused such a battle?

within our souls lurks a danger
which if aroused will seek its rest in war
as in the village below
where people have lost themselves in the mélee

self-righteousness raised its ugly head
the screams of the right against the righter
two churches plotting
to rid themselves of the other
soon the whole village would be consumed

The smoke and dust rose in the air and mixed with the morning dew. The church of the Saturday Worshipers was engulfed in flames. The men on horseback sat back and watched their handiwork—men of church of the Sunday Worshipers.

The village was now officially at war with itself.

I did not want to admit the awful truth: that the moods of war had been aroused over a disagreement between two religious groups and how they chose to believe in God. That they held their beliefs with such conviction that in their zeal they'd lost all perspective. But the burning building was clear evidence.

Over the years there were always a few zealots who felt it was their mission to tell others which was the "right" day to worship God, but nothing ever went beyond an occasional heated argument. The puzzle now was how such an argument had become so riled that it had acted as a trigger, causing one group to set fire to another group's place of worship . . . to declare war.

buildings can burn in an hour and turn to ash
but the greater danger is the fire in our souls
that may not be quenched

a fire that burns from within has not limits
who can stop us when we are bent on destroying
because of the resentments we have held within?

As I watched the church burn, I felt the need to persuade the people to stop their fighting. I began my descent into the village, my thoughts already in the village, not upon my feet and the loose rocks beneath them. Suddenly I lost my footing and stumbled, tumbling about two hundred feet down the slope. I do not know how long I lay there unconscious, but it was long enough for the sun to begin to shade the other side of the trees. As I awoke I remembered my dream about being a child playing with other children of the village.

In the dream, we invited anyone who wanted to play with us to join the games, excluding no one based on religion, race, or gender. We judged solely on the willingness to play fairly, for if someone did not play fairly we were uncomfortable and unsure how to respond. Most of us were willing to forgive and forget in these cases, however, and reiterate that all we asked was to "do no harm."

> *where is the answer to self-righteous anger?*
> *who has the wisdom to stop us?*
>
> *perhaps the answer lies where no words are written*
> *where no person has to be taught.*
>
> *many a nation has been destroyed*
> *when no wise men were found*
>
> *where are the village's wise men?*
> *where are the answers for the fury of war?*
>
> *should we not turn to the wise children*
> *instead of the adults who engage in the battle?*

As these thoughts of my childhood and my dream faded, my awareness of the current situation returned. My ankle was throbbing and swelling quickly; I must have sprained or broken it. I lay on the rocks, barely conscious, while the village people below continued to explode with

rage and hate for one another. Though I was too injured
to stand and continue my journey down the slope to the
village, I kept thinking about how much I needed to get
there and that if I only could I would stop the war—if only
they would listen.

But there I lay, unable to move, in the rubble of
gravel. Gradually my mind began to shake its unconscious
state and I realized then it was madness for me to think I
could avert this war, and hence my attention now returned
to my own misfortune. The fall had hurt my ankle, it had
ballooned, and I could not move it.

While I lay on the hillside, wounded by my own
carelessness and feeling faint again, my anxiety grew for
my village, at war with itself. I lay back in frustration. As
I did I saw two figures coming toward me. Relieved, I
waited. An elderly man and a young boy approached and
stopped in front of me, then bent down to examine me.

I am vague about exactly what happened next. I
believe the old man told the boy to hold my head in his lap
while he made a bed from small tree branches. Then they
placed me on the bed and proceeded to carry me down the
hill and into the village.

I began to dream again of my childhood. In my dream
a close friend was told not to play with me anymore
because he was now old enough to "know better." His
parents believed in God differently from my parents, and
so my friend was required to terminate his friendship
with me. It was at that point that the concept of "fair play"
began to fade and new boundaries were set based on what
we were taught about what constituted "friendship."

When I suddenly awoke from this dream-state
consciousness, it was from the intense pain of my injury.
I watched from the make-shift bed as the elderly man and

the young boy carried me past the burning church. I raised
my head a bit, noting that the people were standing by
helplessly, as the fire could not be put out. It was curious
how the elderly man and the boy hardly acknowledged the
fire at all, walking with their heads down as they delivered
me down the street.

why do dreams bring answers?
why do memories conceal the truth?

why does pride not learn from the past?
why does God allow us to fight over spiritual truths?
why are the moods of war in all of us?

why is the solution so near us and yet so far?
why can't we learn before it is too late?

The man and the boy took me to a part of the village
where I had hardly ventured before—a general store.
They knocked on the door in the back. A middle-aged
couple opened the door and immediately let us in. I hardly
knew this couple, for they were not of my own religious
persuasion and I had never been allowed in their store. But
here I was now, a person in need of help, and here they
were, willing to provide aid. After the elderly man and the
young boy lay me on a bed they left me with the couple. I
learned that the couple was childless and that their general
store was very big and had more products than the general
store I had always visited.

They told me that the building that burned was the
church of the Saturday Worshipers, an act of retaliation
by the Sunday Worshipers for blocking the road to
the Sunday Worshipers' church. Then they told me
something I did not know. It seems the road to the Sunday

Worshipers' church passed through a section of private land and that land belonged to one of the Saturday Worshipers. That the easement through the property had always been honored with a verbal agreement, but a new decision regarding the easement had been made.

They continued the story, saying that historically it had always been recognized that there was a right for all to pass through the easement and no one ever questioned that right until the day when a Saturday Worshiper's cart tipped over and a passing Sunday Worshiper did not stop to help and even made some rude remarks as he passed by. He boasted that the Saturday Worshiper was being punished by God for not honoring the Sabbath, that the cart in the mud on a Sunday was proof that one should be in church and not going to market.

As the news leaked out, the owner of the land then decided to block the road to punish the Sunday Worshiper for not stopping to help the Saturday Worshiper with the tipped cart. This meant that the Sunday Worshipers would have to cross the creek to get to their church. Hence had begun the conflict between these two religious factions.

> *the world is grieved when its inhabitants*
> *fight over how to worship God*
>
> *how is it that when and how we worship*
> *has come to have more sway than our actions*
>
> *how did we take fair play and*
> *manifest self-righteousness*

Soon other smaller groups of God-believing people were taking sides and a bigger fight began to brew. After I heard the couple's story about the initial impetus for the arson, I felt more confused and helpless as to what I could do to stop this fighting.

As I thought about my village's history, and the impending talk of a war between these groups, the couple from the general store tended to my ankle. They were able to reduce the swelling and put a splint on my foot, then offered me crutches until I was healed enough to return them. I thanked the couple profusely and promised to return the crutches. I was about to leave their store when I remembered the elderly man and the young boy. I asked the couple about them, and if the boy was possibly the elderly man's grandson.

They said the boy was of no relation to the elderly man and neither had family in this village. The boy had simply appeared one day and had begun tagging along with the man. As long as the boy caused no trouble, the villagers were content with the arrangement. Indeed, I had seen them occasionally in the village, but they never stayed long and I'd never given them much thought until now. But now I wondered where the man came from and why he cared for the young boy. At that moment the man and the boy returned to the general store to check on me. They asked me not to tell anyone that they had helped me, for the boy belonged to a family with eleven other children in another village.

The elderly man said he did not want any unnecessary talk of him or the boy, for the boy was a blessing to him. He said, "Me and the boy just help others in need. As the boy is as willing as I am to help others, we seem to understand each other well."

Then they told me the news from the town, that the rumors of a war were true and that the men of the village had decided to meet for a fight at the "Old Meadow," about half a mile south of the village. For years the Old Meadow, as it was called (although no one knows why), had been the neutral ground where the children played — until their parents told them they were not allowed to go there anymore. Now it was about to become a battleground for the adults. The elderly man and young boy left after giving us this news.

I was very grateful to the couple at the general store and to the elderly man and the young boy. Now I needed to return to my own house and start gathering information about the fight that continued to percolate. Before I left, the couple told me they had prayed very diligently for this fight not to happen, and that they wondered if God ever answered prayers like this one, for there was a long history of these kinds of wars everywhere. They said that though they had prayed they could not see how this war could be stopped. I agreed with them, and told them I too was wondering the same thing.

I left the store and hurried home the best I could on the crutches. I gathered what news I could about town, where everyone was asking everyone else to take sides. I refused, retreating to the top of the hill with a backpack now full of supplies that I thought would last me a few days.

By the time I reached the top of the hill my ankle was throbbing again and the pain was even greater than before. I had not listened to the advice of the couple from the general store — to stay off the foot — and I was now sorry. But I was alone with my thoughts, and it seemed this was where I needed to be to try to discern the real reason for the fight in the village below. I needed an answer, but sensed that though I might have had one once, now it was lost.

where is our childhood when we need it most?
taught to put away childish things
we pick up the mature stuff of life
and are soon without a map

has God given us the childish things
to take with us into our adult life?
has "fair play" been written into us with the words
treat others as you want them to treat you?

I made a seat of grass and sat down, settling myself on top of the hill for a clear view of the village and the Old Meadow. Tears rolled down my face, for an anger was rising in me. I felt my own intolerance of both these groups, knowing I was like them and having to admit to myself I did not have an answer either. As I was thinking this, my thoughts were interrupted by loud horns blasting, horns customarily used for alerting the village people of emergencies. I heard the horns well upon this hill, and then began to see movements of the village men, who seemed to be forming into two separate groups at the edge of the Old Meadow.

I do not know exactly why they agreed to meet in that spot. Perhaps it was to spare the village from more destruction. Perhaps it was because the Old Meadow had always been considered the one place of neutral ground.

I heard shouts and horns coming from every direction and I felt the restlessness of the men below. Some were on horses and the rest were on foot, and all were rearing their heads, ready for battle.

And then, a most unexpected event occured.

how is it that we measure faith?
why do we imagine that God takes sides with our cause?
it seems God intervenes little in our affairs
though we imagine otherwise

so we war with each other
and God appears not to stop us
but could God be active in our lives
by what He writes upon our souls?

is it up to God whether we see or do not see
His involvement in our lives?
if so it is no wonder we are willing to fight in this way

Suddenly, from the small brushy areas that surrounded parts of the Old Meadow, the children of the village emerged and began charging into the center of the meadow with wooden swords and spears. Shocked, I could only imagine the surprise and fright the men were experiencing at that moment.

The men instinctively froze as the children ran toward them. Perhaps the men feared that if they moved they might start a battle and that in the confusion the children would be harmed or even killed. I believe that each of these men was concerned about his own children or grandchildren, and none wanted to be the cause of a more serious event that would harm his own. So they stood and watched the children until, about thirty minutes later, the children dropped their wooden swords and began playing other games.

For a while the men seemed rooted to the spot, unable to move, but soon they became restless and decided to try to scatter the children away. As they did, however, another event occurred that was equally as unexpected.

I could now see the elderly man and the young boy who had helped me earlier pushing a cart full of what looked like toffee-covered apples into the center of the meadow. As soon as the children saw the cart they rushed up to it, and the man and the boy began passing out the candied fruits. The children were laughing and playing, and again the men were stunned and rooted to the spot.

all are welcome here
please join in
we play from a source
from within

we mean none harm
we enjoy the hours of the day

this is how we make friends
this is how we keep friends

From my perch at the top of the hill I could see that the men continued to watch the children in the meadow, and that something odd was beginning to happen. Even from this distance, I could sense the men's anger was diminishing. Sure enough, several of the men began to disperse — with grins on their faces! I understood immediately that it was difficult for them not to feel pleasure in watching their children at play, and in that pleasure forget the reason they were there in the first place. Just then I even heard a few of them laughing.

Suddenly a third unexpected event occurred as the children's mothers came running into the meadow from all directions and began gathering up their children. In a span of about thirty minutes, the old meadow was cleared of all the children and not a sound could be heard. But what few men were left seemed to have lost all desire for war.

moods of war
you cowered to the children of fair play
how will we live with ourselves without war?
how is it a few children hold the power to change
the dreadful fate of the moods of war within?

some say it was miracle of God's making
others say it was a miracle of the children's making

I began my descent from the hill shortly after the men left the Old Meadow. I hobbled back to my house and went to bed early due to my developing fever. I did not stir for a few days and in time my ankle began to heal.

The couple from the general store visited me twice during this time and left some food. They told me that the elderly man and the young boy, who were leaving the area for another part of the region, wanted to wish me good health.

war and peace can be made in a day
but the consequences can last forever

may the memories of this day burn upon our souls forever
may we learn the value of fair play
and pass it along to the next generation

~

As the village people retell this story over time, I have never heard the elderly man and the young boy mentioned, nor their gift of the toffee-covered apples in the meadow. It was as if it had never happened. But I knew what I'd seen and found it strange that the men spoke about the children and how their mothers came to fetch them, but failed to recognize the man, the boy, or their role in ending the war. I remembered a time a few years before when I'd alerted a family after spotting their boat drifting away from the shore and assisted them in retrieving the boat before it got too far away. A few days after the boat incident, when I spoke of it to them, I was surprised that they did they not recall me at all, only that their boat had drifted and they had gone after it.

I was puzzled by the fact this family did not remember me, but I know that sometimes the unexpected can cause us to miss important facts. In this way, perhaps the men that day in the Old Meadow were so bewildered by the events and so engrossed with the children's behavior that the appearance of an old man and a young boy with toffee-covered apples did not register. That is my guess, anyway.

After some time passed, it was agreed that the whole village would assist the Saturday Worshipers in the rebuilding of their church. The road to the church was soon reopened. It was also decreed by the town that everyone from the village was required to help anyone who happened to be stranded on the road, no matter what day it was. For a while, the village was renewed.

As time went on, tensions concerning religious beliefs occasionally stirred up again in the village, but never to the same degree as during the incident that is now referred to as the "Old Meadow War."

> *does a story end when our interest ends*
> *if so it would be wise to read on*
> *for this story has more length yet*

A few years later the couple from the general store shared the following information about that day, something I had not known. They recounted to me that the elderly man had sent word by the young boy to all the children of the village that he planned to give away a whole cart full of candied toffee apples, and that all they had to do was to meet him in the Old Meadow, stage a "play battle," and then wait until he came with the fruit.

The couple told me they had supplied the apples and the toffee and the recipe, and that the four of them then had a very busy morning making so many treats. I told them I had always thought it was a miracle that the children had appeared when they did and diverted the war, but now, upon hearing this news, I was not sure it had been a true miracle. Had not the old man coaxed the children to come to the meadow?

I told them I was disappointed because I liked thinking that somehow the children had simply shown up on their own, as if God had drawn them. The woman from the general store said, "Well, I believe it was a miracle that the war was diverted, and if God used an elderly man, a young boy, a middle-aged couple, and toffee-covered apples to do it, that is just part of the miracle."

life does not always go as we expect
it takes many turns as we live it

but in the end — hopefully —
we have all learned our lessons well

it was the unexpected play of the children
that saved the day and perhaps a few lives as well

if this is true then learn the lesson well
for surprises like the children's fair play
are full of wisdom worth remembering

At first I continued to be upset that the elderly man had tempted the children into the old meadow, knowing there was a war about to start. I had questions, too: How did this elderly man know that the children's actions would stop the war? Did he have the secret to understanding our nature? But since he had gone I knew I might never know the answers. Sometimes I even wonder if the elderly man existed at all, but the couple from the general store keep telling me that, in fact, he did. Either way, I do believe that the actions of this elderly man saved the village and that the village remains altogether unaware.

Will the mysteries of life ever cease?

The Old Meadow is still there at the outskirts of the village, and it is still referred to as the "neutral ground," a place where the children can go and play and discover fair play — that is, until their parents tell them it's time to stop going to the Old Meadow and start learning about God.

will we ever rid ourselves of the fatal flaw
not accepting other beliefs as equal to our own?

is God content to allow us
to work out our quarrels on our own?

is fair play God's way of giving us a way out?
and if so is fair play inherent in us?

it cannot be denied that we abandon fair play with age
and that children are our reminders of its wisdom

People in the village continue to talk about the Old Meadow War, as if to remind themselves of the event. I first heard the phrase in the general store where I shop for my weekly goods. I then heard it in a local saloon and then even heard it in a Sunday morning sermon. But when I heard the phrase sung by the children in a song they had written that I was brought sobbing to my knees.

The song made it clear that the children knew all along they were headed for danger, that they knew they were taking a risk, but that possibly it was the only option for stopping their parents' war. Did the old man share this knowledge with the children, and trust them with it?

As I reflect upon the bravery of these children on that day, upon the fact that children were able to stop a war, the enormity of the miracle grows in my mind and soul. The village people may refer to the event as the Old Meadow War, but I refer to it as "the day the children taught the grown-ups the lesson of the wisdom of fair play."

The Old Meadow War Song

meet me at the old meadow
for some apples and toffee
what do you say?

let's all go to the old meadow
to laugh and run and do tricks
and play

do not tell your mothers
where you are going
come now and do not slam the door

who believes us that we are
going to the old meadow to
stop a war

our fathers watched us behind the trees
and as strange as it may be
we the children came to play
so our fathers would not die that day

meet me at the old meadow
for some apples and toffee
what do you say?

Part Two:
Moods of War Rhapsody

Rhapsody: Moods of War (1)

First Daydream

1.
I am the moods of war
You are my servant
With your vanity of beliefs
You think you know best
but you are only as a waft caught in my laughter

    I lead you always to the brink of war
    You are my sure bet
    You are the drink of life for me
    I am the drink of death for you

        I came to make a treaty with you
        and you agreed
        Now I have the power and I have the right
        You must bow and you must fight

This is your confession in your own words to the world
These words were formed not by your lips but by your life

    I have given my allegiance to this power that wants to rule
    over me
    and wants me to rule over others
    I will give everything to have it come true
    I will give my friends . . . my wife . . . my children

        And the "war" of this power that lives in me
        I count as virtue
        But in truth I fear it is the ultimate sin
        and I am bound by it

For the power of the moods of war is master over me
I am enslaved to fight to win until I lose
Within my soul the moods of war
live and breathe.

2.
I come disguised as your servant and your friend
I come cloaked in peace and I am its price
I am of the fountain of your conscience
I water Your reason and your heart
So drink now for your enemy is also mine

The moment you dreamed of being first
is the moment you caved in
You took your hand in mine and together
we have become the moods of war

I am the place of no rest
The giver of pride
with righteousness greed and
love of self mixed in

If there is one God and if God is lax
I can do as I please
I live to consume you
to live out my own "fall" through you
God is after my soul and you are my shield

You are as useful to God as a speck of dust on a rock
but to me you are my protection
For the God I have offended
has allowed me to use you and the earth as a
battleground

I am the error of God's creation
I am the duality of good and evil
For He and I are at war
and that is the bigger picture

From my lips I confess —
the moods of war is my temper
I will have my way with it
and with the earth before I fall
And I will take you
with me

Your fall is my glory.

3.

Who am I and what am I that I would have breath
and that I have breathed in you and brought you to action?

What entity of God am I that I would have power
over you and what power is this that God does not
interfere with or contend with on the earth?

So are we left on earth
to grapple with the power of war without aid of God
Why am I allowed to live in you and offer you no relief?
What does it all mean in the bigger scheme of things?

4.

Who is it who sees the people of earth as those with
pain and tears? Who is it who does not interfere in the
affairs of humans even at great expense? Who is it who
passes along the message as to how to keep the peace, and
yet allows us to conceive the moods of war in our hearts
and minds and spirits and does nothing to stop it?

In your heart, mind, and spirit I have conceived a belief in you that has grown and taken root.

You conceive in your being that you have come to the knowledge of the one and only true way to God. Now I will have my way with you, and I will guide you through your folly.

How many times will you be let down and go uncleansed? How long will it take for you to see that it is your image of God that makes you vulnerable to this war within?

To believe in war as a means of lasting peace is like believing that God has created you so that He may answer your prayers and thereby prove His existence to you.

He who becomes your friend can also become your enemy, for before morning comes the world can change.

So in you I will reign, because fear of all shadows leads you into my light. Who am I in you that would cause you this fight?

Rhapsody: Moods of War (2)

Second daydream

1.

The wise who offer reliable and good counsel place themselves not in any person's plan. Though we may walk the way of the wise and cause not the war we may still be shackled with making the peace.

>*thus are the straps of the moods of war*
>*we are engaged in the battle for our soul*
>*so wise or not . . . it is off to war we go.*

Are we willing to live with it and balance on a tight rope as we lead? Is there a wisdom that can balance all nations and leaders? Will there be a day when we do not look into the eyes of this God? If there is, it will be the same day we stop looking in the mirror for an image of God.

Though we may not start wars, we may have to learn to be ready for them, for it seems as long as earth remains wars will be.

the righteousness with which we are born
is the arena where the trap is laid
and the bait is set
for it is there
where hearts minds and spirits
are tested.

2.

Can the power of the moods of war be quenched? Why
cannot we see that their war cannot be won?

> *if victory runs into the arms of the mighty*
> *if we believe we are the mighty*
> *then it is precisely the war every person wants*

This kind of theology of peace on earth always
requires someone's blood. Why would the real God of the
earth require blood and sacrifice in exchange for peace?

3.

As long as the moods of war have their place on earth,
though you may not want to war with your neighbor, your
neighbor may want to war with you.

> *can any of us cower to the moods of war*
> *are these spiritual entities so real*
> *that they demand us to fight?*

> *if we choose not to fight*
> *are we their prey?*
> *whether we fight or not*
> *either way are we their prey?*

Is it our nature to war, and as such something we
must live with? There is no clear answer and there is no
clear villain, but there we are the victims.

If I am a pawn or a failure of the human race, I will
take my fate on my knees and bow to God. No matter
what the plan, God is the ultimate reality. If war is within
me and I have no way out, if God is the ultimate reality

and if this is God's way, then I will bow and wait for the plan to play itself out.

Whether we are pawns or failures of God, or failures of our own making, God's mercy must be in the plan and the way out. No one's dignity is lost when God is supreme; since we cannot change what is in us and it is our destiny to war, our destiny must be God's design. Therefore, I must submit.

4.

God, could you tell me now, if I only defend myself, am I in the wrong in this war? Stay with me awhile and see what unfolds. . . . Where is the mercy of God?

if i fight then i fight only as a defense
why must i wait until i die to see
what the final outcome will be?

If the mercy of God is found in His silence, though I struggle against the moods of war within myself and battle this duality of good and evil, God is with me. So, in my wait is my hope also — that I am set free at my death.

5.

If in God's mercy we are all judged equally regardless, then is it only on earth that we are held prisoner by this power, a power that seeks to own us and plant roots of divisions amongst us? If this is so, then it is indeed good news, for at my death I will be free of it.

this vision is a breath of fresh air
to believe that God ultimately takes
responsibility for earth and all its inhabitants

i journey onward with the belief
that man cannot offend God
and live with the moods of war as best i can

their power has hold of me till i leave
my last breath knowing that evil cannot follow me
beyond the grave i am relieved
i bow to my God
forever thankful that my battle stays here

The question is not whether the bull with the horns has been tamed, or whether the horns have been shaved, for questions like these have no answer, but my question to me is whether I am at peace with my fate.

Rhapsody: One Woman Said

One young woman said, "I do not want to think of the negative, only the positive." I do not know what she meant by this, but her comment referenced this writing, as if it were wrong to voice the thoughts and ask the questions.

The woman implied that our attacks on other people's beliefs should not be questioned, and then she added these words, emphatically, "Christians have that right."

The woman's husband told me he does not see God the way I do as evidenced by these writings--and nor does God, he added. Therefore I must be deranged to write about God in this way, and need a "more solid Christian foundation." As he spoke, the man's rage rose in him with great righteousness, his rage the proof that he was righteous and had God's approval.

And so it was that I was the target of his rambling ire as the moods of war in him were let loose.

But this man was not done and further "explained" that true compassion is what is demonstrated by anyone who makes the effort to convert others to his belief. In other words, that not attempting to convert others means we will be judged and punished for it eternally.

In my mind, this man is the kind of man to whom this poetry speaks.

After this conversation our friendship waned quickly.

Or should I say, fell off a cliff.

Rhapsody: Kings of War

1.

Men like him dream of being king
He knows in his heart it is meant to be
He has seen his image in the mirror
He has licked the hand that feeds his fear

He believes it is the hand of God
and the company he keeps agrees
They should look no further
for to this man they will attach their wagon
as they too have licked the hand of the dragon

Thoughts of barns full of wealth
make them drunk with greed
A vain man admires these kinds of wagons
and believes the wagons were made for his own
use He encourages others to attach their dreams to
his He knows in his heart it is meant to be

For men like him have seen a vision
and ride at the front of a great chariot
chanting, "We are chosen by a force
that has taken our soul for a
possession
We are the Kings of War with an appetite
satisfied only by the offering of a sacrifice."

from the womb to the tomb
hear the mothers cry
You take from my birth and return it to the earth
from the womb to the tomb
the fathers ask why

Men like him believe their dreams are of God
the same God who made them king
They announce to the world that it is their calling
that through them all will have a right to be free

So the rage of wars begin
wars fought for money and the rights to it
man against man killing for rights such as this

The beast of war busily devours each man
shouting the same words again and again
"Slay each other for your souls are the food I demand"

All the while the men lick the feet
of the riders of the great chariots
and in their sleep breathe hard and dream on
shouting in unison with the beast of war
"We have become the Kings of War
We are the rulers as in our dreams
We are the willing to be counted among the thieves
We know not that we are to be judged
by our thoughts or our deeds"

> *from the womb to the tomb*
> *hear the mothers cry*
> *You take from my birth and return it to the earth*
> *from the womb to the tomb*
> *the fathers ask why.*

2.

They ready the wagons to be filled
It is a merchant's dream to find strangers
willing to die for the merchant's full wagon
merchants who have found the key to men's souls
"Make them believe we are looking after them

and always repeat to them it is God's will"
Men who reason with themselves that
they were made for this purpose
that the land they rule was made for this reason

The leaders of the band of thieves give speeches
"If your sons and daughters die for this reason
I will mourn with you for I am Commander In Chief
and all the company I keep agrees"
But a thought remains unspoken —

His wagons need to be filled
and all kings need men like you to fill them

The hour is always at hand
as the war room makes its plan
The shadows of death
shall have it all before it rests
The Kings of War
will now lick the hand of the beast
Nations are lined up for the blood feast

And all this for one drink of the black wine
One taste and you will want it all
Men like this walk the halls in the nations of the free
believing it is their destiny
to give all nations their dream
as if all dreams of import are from them who rule

As the breath of the dragon whispers
"All needy souls have a fee and homage to pay to me"

from the womb to the tomb
hear the mothers cry
You take from my birth and return it to the earth

from the womb to the tomb
the fathers ask why.

3.

Do you not see the mountain of heaven where hell resides
where the fallen angels are tied
From the distant mountain I hear the shout

> "I am the God of War
> I come to you in the night with a dream
> To you I am a god
> Now I tell you plainly I do not lie
> I want all your sons and daughters to die
> Sacrifice their lives to me
> Bow to the belief
> That all strangers have the right to be free
> All the while I know it is mine to give for a fee"

The castle of power is ready to spit its fire
to feed the glory of the Kings of War
There is a legend that says men like these
peer down from their towers
blind to see that their glory will pass in a single hour
But the rocks of their castle are built by the greed
of the spirits of the gods bound up on the mountain

And these gods blind men with greed as if it were a virtue

These are the angels of God that left Him
Now their castles of earth fall
by their own power and greed
the Kings of War swallowed by their own fire

Empires are falling by the hands of the angels of God who
are bound
the rubble covered by the tears of sorrow of the mothers
and fathers who give their sons to this horror as if an
honor

As the flames engulf their sons
and until the flame goes out
the Kings of War hope there is no God
for no God means no shame to share

Men are consumed in the song of the dragon
dancing every chance chanting "I have done
no wrong for I have dreamed of being a king
and I kissed the palm of the serpent
for one chance for the world to bow before me and repent"

So . . . legend or no the truth is still the truth:
That men like him bow to a power that overwhelms
and seek the wealth of the world as their own
whatever it takes to make people their slaves

> *from the womb to the tomb*
> *hear the mothers cry*
> *You take from my birth and return it to the earth*
> *from the womb to the tomb*
> *the fathers ask why.*

4.

Where are your wagons
and to which king did you hitch your wagon
You will weep with others like you
when your wagons are taken from you

For the houses of the wealthy are full of your wagons
there is no protection
only credit to fill your stomachs
It will cost you all your years
to undo what the Kings of War have done
As you sleep they will arise again
their dreams tied to the gods
as they preach the sacrifices you must make

there will always be men like them and you

The Kings of War have plenty
and so do their friends and their wagons
They chat daily about war and its need:

we need a war to fill our poverty inside

They chop us up and serve us on a platter
Even that will not stop their aching souls' chatter

trade it all for oil they say
it is only our freedom we seek
for we are the voices of these fallen angels
and our chant is to the Kings of War

Chanting louder for all to hear

i am not afraid . . . only a war will do what i need
and i am not afraid to send others to die

So the Kings of War arise as if they are the voice of God

where is the mirror? they say
i must look at myself again
to keep my image fresh in my mind

i must see myself as a king
so when i am amongst the crowd
they will bow and i will scarce hear their cry

from the womb to the tomb
hear the mothers cry
You take from my birth and return it to the earth
from the womb to the tomb
the fathers ask why.

Part Three:
The Tunnel Dreams

Tunnel Dreams (dreams of the soul)

1.

i am aware i am dreaming
when i hear a voice
"you must choose . . . choose a tunnel"

I do not know what the voice means
Then I see me standing at the entrance to a cave
I know it is the entrance to my soul
that beyond lies four tunnels

an ancient garden is in front of the cave
appearing long abandoned
at its center a dry fountain

I thought my soul was nonexistent
a figment of my imagination
But now in my dream I see it is vast
and mysterious and real with tunnels

my body, heart, and mind race with confusion
are these the tunnels from which i must choose
what do these tunnels mean?
why must i make a choice?
who and what is this voice?

My soul is like an unexplored cave
with tunnels of beliefs and the choices I have made
the choices of life

are these the tunnels collected by my spirit?
is my soul the place for storing everything my spirit collects?

I stand at the entrance of my soul
I enter curious about the nature of the tunnels
my soul has formed
I am timid yet eager to see what is inside me
to see what choices of belief I have formed
Then fear overshadows my thoughts for it seems
the choice of tunnel is up to me

Full of questions I contemplate and a light comes on
The more questions I have the path is illuminated
so I keep asking:

> *how do we explore our souls*
> *through the spirit*
> *through the heart*
> *through the mind*
> *. . . or all three*

Questioning brings me further into my soul
where I can sense the presence of my spirit

Does this mean that the journey into the soul
starts by asking questions?
Is it with this effort that our path alights
allowing us to see what is next?

Confused I know only that there is so much
we do not understand
But soon my eyes are drawn to the cavern wall
Four signs clear in the dark . . . the four tunnels

A chill runs up and down my spine
knowing this is the first choice I must make
before the journey into my soul begins

I know that somewhere within my soul
God can be found
It is this thought that lures me in
to search for God within myself
I know it is taking the journey and
searching for the voice calling me in the dream that matters

I enter into the dark cavern of my soul
God's light guiding me to take the first steps.

    2.
Do I dare take the risk
to enter any one of the tunnels
I know I must as the voice cannot be ignored
and I am urged to take my soul's journey again

I look more closely and see that the tunnels vary:

*Tunnel one: solid rock and steel; an ancient, beautiful garden
with a dry fountain in its center, resembling the garden outside
the entrance of my soul; Tunnel two: highly decorative, ornate,
and sensual, with weapons of many types strewn about; Tunnel
three: a wide entrance, asymmetrical in form, with hundreds of
books on tables and shelves; and Tunnel four: plain, yet superior
in craftsmanship compared to the others, "clean and neat" the
expression that comes to mind*

I keep hearing the voice
the one that comes from my soul
not content to rest
    "You must choose . . . choose a tunnel"

*Tunnel one . . . "there is only one way to the true God and it
starts here. . . ."*

The haunting voice urges me on
Though I know these tunnels I am hesitant to choose
but soon choose the first because it is the one
with which I am most familiar
I enter with the sense that I know it already
for it is where I have lived
but find that the reality of my past experience has
somehow not allowed me to see what I now see
I am confused for I thought I knew this tunnel well
but it is as if I am seeing it for the first time

My observations are coming fast and my heart is racing
The ceilings are so low I have to bow my head as I walk
The light is dim and conceals bags of trash piled one upon
the other and pushed up against the walls of the tunnel
in huge mounds

> *why are the ceilings hewn so low as to*
> *force one to bow when walking through*
> *what do the trash bags mean*
> *what else is in this tunnel*
> *and what have i missed in me all these years*

Then I am startled
what I see next truly confounds my wits
I am now in a cavernous room with three more tunnels
leading away from it with signs over each one reading:
"Christianity," "Islam," and "Judaism"
I see a multitude of smaller tunnels with
names above them
some I recognize and some not
and branching off from these three larger tunnels

again, the voice from within my soul beckons me forward
calling "you must choose one; choose a tunnel"

I enter the tunnel of Christianity first
It does not take long to see the many other tunnels
branching off it and other smaller tunnels branching off
those branches . . . like the body's veins, arteries, and
capillaries
All the tunnels have names of the Christian denominations
and sects
There is no clear direction and hundreds of options
all leading to more tunnels with more names

I am disturbed by what I see before me
tunnels like mazes with intersections that merge and
collide into each other
tunnels once dug and forgotten
tunnels that have caved in and lead nowhere
a giant labyrinth without exit or end

> *why – what is the meaning*
> *what is my soul telling me*
> *what truth lies in the tunnel where the sign reads*
> *"there is only one way to the true God and it starts here"*

> *i am unnerved at my discoveries in the Christian tunnel*
> *will i ever understand the meaning of the trash*
> *the low ceilings the dim lights and the multitude*
> *of endless tunnels*

A darkness overcomes me and I cannot see
until more questions surface and the light returns

I am now inside the tunnel of the sign that reads "Islam"
and then in the tunnel of "Judaism"

both similar to the "Christianity" tunnel
and then I am in all three tunnels simultaneously

> *how can these three tunnels be the same*
> *is the answer in the title of main tunnel, which reads:*
> *"there is only one way to the true God and it starts here"*

A nagging feeling reveals
that these three tunnels lead to nowhere
that all the tunnels are in conflict
at war with all the others

Has the search for God made us warriors
and has God become a warrior God?

As this revelation occurs I am drawn to the darker corners
of the tunnels
where I see weapons of all kinds waiting to be used
as if the tunnels needed weapons

I stumble out of the tunnels
horrified by what I've seen
afraid of what it means
I recall what else I saw . . . the three larger tunnels
and all the other smaller ones digging into each other
evidence of a struggle at each site drawn on the walls
records of continual wars waged

I cannot choose a tunnel
and so I leave
yet the voice keeps calling me
telling me to choose.

3.

I stand in the main cavern staring at the four signs
feeling the urgency to enter the second tunnel
the one that reads *"Beyond this point there is no God"*

My observations come quickly
—high ceilings dim light trash everywhere—
like the first tunnel—but stacked not bagged
and formed into tables benches and chairs . . .
and weapons

I walk through into a large cavern much like the first
this one resembles a huge nightclub
the smell of perfume and deodorants hanging in the air
as if to mask the rancid smell
I peer into the tunnels shooting off from this cavern
and wrinkle my nose
they all smell of death and of rotting bodies
weapons are strewn about—swords and lances and shields
I know the two tunnels are at war with each other and
themselves
Cruelty and anger are palpable against all those unwilling
to join the fight.

I return to the "lounge" and then venture into a few of the
side tunnels
small ones unfinished or abandoned or caved in
Why does this tunnel treats its trash differently?
Why are the tunnels at war?

As I contemplate I become aware that I have been in this
tunnel before
I am not comfortable and am not content to stay
I do not trust this club atmosphere of the cavern and sense
the rafters are faulty as well

Then the voice comes again
"Hedonism is considered no crime here
war is no crime either
The only crime is being disloyal to the tunnel"

But what is the warning I am supposed to hear?
What is the danger that lurks?
Why am I stuck in this dream of tunnels and choice?

I am sweating profusely by now
for I both do and do not want to be here
I know this tunnel is in me and that I cannot deny it
I can only try to avoid chosing it.

      4.
Suddenly I have passed out
I see myself being carried on a stretcher into the third
tunnel above which the sign reads
"God-believers with no rules other than that enter here."
Like the other two tunnels there is trash
this time carelessly swept into the darker recesses of the
cavernous space and up against the walls
Through one of the spoke tunnels I find myself in a great
library
where other tunnels lead to learning about science, art,
war, business, philosophy, and religion

The ceilings are high and the tunnels isolated
as if absorbed by their own interests
One large room is like a bank for exchanging money and
goods
Each room's harmony depends on what takes place in it

I fear this tunnel most of all
as it appears to have no interest in anything else but its

own endeavors
as if it were the tunnel of many Gods
It is a selfish tunnel—
not necessarily violent or hedonistic—
but without rules
without empathy

> *i fear this existence yet know it is in my soul*
> *that my soul has formed this tunnel*
> *that I am being asked to choose it or another*
> *the voice does not care which tunnel i choose*
> *but only that i make the choice*

> *i try to run but am suddenly crippled*
> *unable to stand i am then carried out*
> *the same way i was carried in.*

5.

Transported from the tunnel
I have a dream within my dream
I see within the third tunnel the great buildings
of the world first as ancient structures to God
that over time have become buildings for
commerce and trade

As the buildings fade I see myself standing in the main
cavern in front of the fourth tunnel
I know I must enter this tunnel with the sign that says
"We all worship the same God"
And the voice imparts its mantra yet again: *"You must
choose a tunnel"*

This structure is plain and well constructed
its craftsmanship superior to the others
it is neat and clean as far as I can see

Each step I take I expect to see the same garbage I'd seen in
the other three main tunnels
to my surprise there is none

I am puzzled by what I do see
small fires like campsites along the walls
the areas around them swept clean
Where is the trash?

The ceiling is not too high
I can reach up and touch it with my hand
After a long walk I finally come to a room with many
branches and am stunned when I see that these tunnels
have many of the same names as the first tunnel—
Christianity, Islam, Judaism, and many other religions
I venture into several long ones
all leading to the same room where a kiva fireplace sits
in the center complete with fire burns and the engraved
words: *"Treat others as you want them to treat you . . . for we
are all seeking the same God"*

I like this tunnel
What does this kiva fireplace mean?
Why is it the only one?
I see ghostlike figures approaching the kiva and filling it
full of trash which is consumed by the fire
a process repeated over and over
as if there is no end to the trash
and the fire can keep up with burning it all away

> *the ghostlike figures remind me of myself*
> *in a flash i see these figures as my*
> *body my mind and my heart*

Suddenly the room with the fireplace disappears
I am whisked into a space with no walls and full of clouds
I am traveling through them into the center of the space
I know where I am going for I come here often
It is the *"Place of Lights"*

These questions are waiting for me:
What is the meaning of the signage the dim lights the
ceiling heights the trash . . . and the tunnels themselves?
Why dream this dream?
I think I know as this is where I go when I seek answers

> *the voice i am hearing i recognize as my spirit*
> *but why i wonder does it speak to me in dreams*
> *and why does it insist that i choose a tunnel?*

6.
I sit with quiet all around me
I have arrived at the place of lights
a place I discovered years ago
first in a dream and then as a place I sought out in my
prayers daydreams and during times of solitude
where my spirit dwells within my soul
It is here that I can begin to understand the meanings
of my questions

I remember the long-abandoned garden
outside the first cave
I know it was at one time very beautiful
and that the dry fountain at its center was once filled
with rushing water
and the meaning begins to unfold
This is the garden of my birth of my innocence of my first
recognition of my soul and spirit
It is the garden whose beauty shifted as my body, mind,

and heart became imperfect as my innocence was lost
It was there that I became intolerant of other people's
discovery of their own souls
and where my intolerance led to the drying up
of my being

When our innocence declines do we begin to seek it again
to dig tunnels in our soul forever in its pursuit?
If so, it would seem that our souls are like caves
and we the carvers of its many tunnels

Suddenly I also remember a tablet of stone, broken, half
covered in weeds, and forgotten in the garden
its inscription, *"There is one God who is the God of all, and
God's mercy is the fate of all the people of the earth."*

I am startled at my recollection and cannot
make out the meaning
but my spirit urges me on to other parts of the dream
so I resettle myself back into the place of lights
and let it unfold

The four main tunnels appear to represent my life's beliefs
the ones formed by my soul and past
I now believe all souls form tunnels like these
*– this is my journey and these are
the tunnels of my soul*

Tunnel one, with its exterior ancient garden,
represents the elusive promises inside, and the dry
fountain represents the failure of the promises of the
tunnel. Although the intentions are good, the promises
still fail. The rock in the architecture around the entrance
represents the hard-core intolerance the believers of this
tunnel have toward others who do not follow them and

the steel is the virtue of the tunnel, which justifies the violent means against any who oppose them.

Tunnel two, with its sensual, decorative entrance and construction of concrete and steel, shows that these tunnels pursue their wants and lusts and their thirst to rule over others with an iron fist.

Tunnel three, with its freeform entranceway and wide door indicates to me that for some almost anything goes, in a place where there is such thing as "wrong." A place that turns God into commerce and commerce into a God. This tunnel wants to "live and let live" with the freedom that comes with few laws. But beware, for the love of money is at its root and its root has no heart.

Tunnel four, with its plain construction and superior craftsmanship represents the kind of life that is clean, content, and well formed. The nondescript entrance is easy to miss at first glance, but inside the dimness encourages us to look within. The ceilings are our view of God: low ceilings mean we see God as imposing and demanding, so we walk with our heads down as if bowing. High ceilings mean we view God as above us but not seen by us. Those just high enough to touch with outstretched hand show us that God is here and can be found – if we do the reaching.

The trash represents the destruction we cause on the earth; what we do with it is a reflection of how we deal with our own shame for this destruction. The question is: what do we do about it?

we can bag it and hide it
we can build with it
we can ignore it (but for how long?)
we can burn it
will the kiva fire rid our souls of the destruction we cause?

if we treat others as we want to be treated
then perhaps we can toss our trash into the kiva

The tunnels are the paths of our beliefs. Our soul forms many paths of beliefs and our spirit calls for us to choose one. We each have the freedom to make this choice, questioning along the way to light the path on our journey.

Suddenly my dream shifts and I am alone. The clouds are moving me out of my dream, so I quickly make this proclamation to myself before it is gone: Today, I choose the path of the fourth tunnel.

As the place of lights slowly fades I am standing beside my bed watching myself sleep. I wake and rise to record my dream. I set the pad on the nightstand, then lie down again, and soon another dream comes.

A Dream of the Mercy of God

1.

cold and wet and chilled to the bone
in front of me stands an image
of me as a young boy

i reach out to touch the image
my hand goes through it
as it would a hologram

from a distance i see light coming
from a cottage in the woods
smoke from the chimney

the image of me suddenly disappears
the cottage lights blink out
the cold and wet and chill return

i feel alone
i know that if something does not change
in my life i will be here forever

i see myself as an old man
who has been walking a long time
with a bag at his side

tired he knows the road we are on
requires us to go on
a little further

we come upon a ridge where the road stops
only sky above and clouds below

the edge of the world
and the end of the road
for me anyway

i knew it was my job to take
what was in the bag
and toss it over the edge

i reach into the bag and take from it my ashes
those of my body, mind, and heart
i toss them over the edge
to be caught by the wind
to scatter

my body mind and heart cease to exist
in that moment
i am now in spirit and truly alive
rid of my body mind and heart
i am now clean and perfect

though spirit is naturally perfect
we will not fully experience it as so
until the body the mind and the heart
cease to be.

2.

i asked "where are you God?
am i not guilty of a crime?
shall i not be judged today"

i was then lifted up in my spirit
to soar above the ridge
and i knew the judgment was "not guilty"
that i was never to be judged

as if God in His mercy does not judge
but takes the blame for the imperfections
of our bodies, hearts, and minds

has it been mercy all along
has God taken my burden upon Himself
is my spirit returning to God?

3.
mercy of God
You do not proclaim me guilty
You ask only that I learn from my spirit
to live on this earth
until it is my time to leave.

Epilogue

I wept when I awoke because I could see our fate on earth is to learn how to live here together. I see now that our spirits are clean before God and that we should not be concerned with death. God has decided our fate after we leave the earth, but has left it to us to decide our fate while we are here. The tunnels in my dream are the paths I choose to take. Humbled by this dream, I weep some more, not for long, but hard, knowing that now I have a faith of my own, one I have come to on my own. I know what I believe and why.

> "There is one God who is the God of all
> God's mercy is the fate of all the people of the earth."

The Night after

In my dream tonight I found myself back in the fourth tunnel where "we all worship the same God." I left and immediately went back to the first tunnel where "there is only one way to the true God and it starts here." As I entered I saw a woman who looked content and satisfied sweeping at the entrance to the Christianity tunnel. She told me this was the only tunnel that mattered in the world. When I asked if she had ever been through the other tunnels, she replied, "The Christianity tunnel is the only tunnel worth entering. It is the tunnel of the one and only true way to God, and it would be immoral to even peek into another tunnel, for God has condemned them all."

No Rest Here

no rest here
only tunneling
pick your God now
for there are many
the one you pick
is the one you will defend

remember
all you have is
a willingness to believe
in the God you choose

i hear this heartfelt confession from many —

my Jesus my God
i now make You and the words of the Bible true
but beyond the next hill there are other men
who have also made heartfelt confessions
to other Gods
who also require obedience to them alone
they command what your God commands
to convert the world and rule

it is confessions like these that chill my soul
because they are many
i ask are we all doomed

> *the fights are many here*
> *and the lights will remain dim*
> *if we learn not how to question.*

The Warrior Gods

1.
the warrior Gods are takers
of our income
our time
our life

The warrior Gods define "sacrifice" as our way to become "right" with God, and they teach that if we do not make the sacrifices required then we cannot become right with God. This belief breeds in them an intolerance of others who do not make the same sacrifices they have made.

It angers them inside, in ways we do not know, when others do not adhere to their beliefs, and it forms in them an intolerant view of us and our beliefs.

They become zealous to convert and to rule and even to war with any who are not willing to believe as they do.

the warrior Gods are takers
of our income
our time
our life

In these ways they are easy to recognize, for they cry, "All are guilty in the name of God who do not bow as we do."

2.
Whether priests, clerics, rabbis, or pastors, they are easy to recognize for they always want our money, our time, our life, and our loyalty — all in the name of God — and it angers them from their depths if we deny them.

it is always about their so-called sacrifice
and our income our time and our life
their view of salvation is for us
to believe in an intolerant God

endless hours of verbal spouting
concerning the sacrifice others
have made on our behalf
our loyalty required in return

And know this: the ones who are doing the speaking are the ones
who are the takers. They can be of any religious name, known
or unknown, all in the "name of God." They are believers in the
warrior Gods and they usurp our right to believe as we want.

It Is No Crime

1.
it is no crime for me to believe in God differently from you
it is amazing to me how eager many are
to proclaim it is a crime

2.
i believe there are many beliefs and paths to God
i believe God allows any path we choose
hopefully we choose the paths that
value the lives of others

i believe closeness to God is evident
by how we treat others
so if many paths can lead us to learn how
— where is the crime in choosing my own path?

Part Four:
Place of Lights

We All Go to Heaven

Though we all go to heaven, we need laws to protect ourselves from each other. Either that or we can learn to place the value on treating others the way we want them to treat us.

Place of Lights

place of lights —
The sensation of being immersed with light
from the inside.

reason being —
God is present on the inside.

the questions —
Does God come from somewhere and enter us?
Is God everywhere all the time therefore manifesting in us?
Why the sensation of light?
Why do we perceive God as appearing in light?
Is the presence of this light within us God's way of making
His presence known?
Can we continue the experience once we are aware of our
spirit within us?
Do we summon the presence of God, or does God decide
to appear regardless?

observation —
This presence of light from the inside is a testimony
about which I have heard and read through the years. It is
not unique to one belief or religion.

the light —
It is not a light in the way we know light, but still a light,
because we have found a part of us that is perfect in every
way, and the knowing of it in us I call the "place of lights."

It Is a Place

it is still and it is quiet
though the world around me
hums with noise

it is a place of lights
not light as the sun
but a light from within
with a new meaning

the light allows me
to see the inside of me
that is of spirit

it is a place i go
where i can choose to go
when i please

my first encounter
was more of a stumbling
than a choice
after that i began to seek
until a path opened

it is still and it is quiet
sensations of light all
around me

if you know of it and have
gone there then the description
is easy to understand.

Place of Lights, 1, 2, and 3

Does God wait upon us to discover God?
What if we do not discover God?
Then what awaits us at the end of our lives?
What is the fate of man?

1.

I remember one day when I was very young, playing alone in a dry creek bed near our house. I was engaged in a conversation with myself when suddenly I looked up, feeling I was being watched. I could not see anyone, but I knew I was being watched and sensed that it was something inside me . . . watching me.

As the years passed, I experienced this often, and the experience slowly became familiar enough that I began to form the belief that it was my spirit keeping watch over me.

But it was during an afternoon nap in my early twenties that I believe I saw my spirit watching me and believed without a doubt that it was indeed my spirit that was staring at me and that I was staring back.

I believe I have visited my spirit many times through the years. My perspective has grown to include the knowledge that our spirit is waiting for us to discover it.

Many speak of a sensation of light when describing the spirit, and I have also had that sensation of light within— not necessarily a light in the physical sense, but rather a light in the form of "knowing" the reality of my spirit, and of my conversing with my spirit in the place of light.

This reality is not easily known . . . and if Jesus' parable about searching and finding had to do with the finding of our spirit, then it is very true indeed.

2.

During an afternoon nap I also saw a beauty in my
spirit; it was without sin or blemish of any kind, and
without need of redemption.

I have reflected many years since on the meaning of
this afternoon nap-dream, and if I have perceived a truth
it is that our spirit is perfect in every way. If this is so, then
we have no need of redemption or salvation because our
spirit goes to heaven at that moment our body dies, the
same moment our mind and heart cease to exist.

I perceive our spirit is full of all the knowledge of God
we need to live on this earth.

I remind myself, here, at this point in life, that I am
still on a journey and that I do not know for sure what is
ahead or what thoughts or events will occur. But I am sure
that if my past is any teacher at all I will more than likely
be forever changing the way I see life, for as long as there
is a road ahead of me there is something new to learn.

3.

Having chosen the fourth tunnel of my dream I go
there often, to the room with the kiva. There I toss in my
trash to learn to treat others as I want them to treat me.

*i want a spirit that is not brutal, or cruel
or intolerant of anything created by God.*

Awareness

I speak of the spirit and the importance of awareness of the spirit; yet as I speak, I often meet people who are kind, people who toil not with the awareness of trauma as I do. So, whether we are aware of our spirit or not, it is the lack of judgment in our soul that reflects that our spirit is awake and at work in us.

> neutrality is the evidence that we do have a spirit
> and neutrality is the way of the spirit.

I Am Without Shame

1.

I am without shame, for my spirit has no sin or flaw in it. I am one with God in the spirit, yet my body, mind, and heart are shamed, for it is there I cannot walk without sin or flaw.

I am with shame because my imperfection guides me down paths of destruction.

I yield to my own belief that my body cannot rid itself of this imperfection, so I seek refuge in my spirit for it can guide me to value all life as equal to my own and as imperfect as my own.

I am therefore transformed and made fit for earth, my spirit waiting for me to die so it can return to God.

2.

Though I live with a burden I am also free from it in the spirit. My body, mind, and heart will decay and my spirit will return to its origin.

3.

Though I may feel shame because of my imperfect body, mind, and heart, God has not made me guilty of eternal crimes. As the imperfection in us is by God's own hand and we are therefore not held guilty of what God has made.

Hence I am eternally without shame.

Thoughts About God

1.

no one knows for sure
the spiritual realm

only by faith do we conceive
of an unseen God

God's book is written in our spirit
man's books are written on paper

no humans become Gods
no Gods become human

God is not partial to any belief, creed, or theology
we all experience the same spiritual realm
the same miracles healings and interventions

God shows all mercy
allows our sins to die with us

then our spirit returns to God
for it is without sin or blemish

i do not know for sure that what i say is absolutely true
but it is what i am willing to believe
and what my faith would have me believe is true . . .
whereby God is mostly silent
and does not much intervene in our lives

> *if God is content to allow this unknowing*
> *concerning our life here and after*
> *then why would God blame*
> *us for questioning it?*

Part Five:

Dream Chronicles (1974-1977)

The Room of My Father

standing atop a hill
i looked up and saw
a message written in the sky

*every fight begins
and ends in the heart*

*we will live and die
according to our heart*

*so do not lose heart
for I will meet you there
in the room of my Father.*

Brick and Steel Are One

I was dropped in the midst of a great city where people were like brick and steel mixed as one, for a war had been underway for some time and destruction was everywhere. It had made the people hard and cold, and though they could see no hope for the future they still struggled to live to their last breath.

> *earth earth where is your God now?*
> *only the altars of fire burn at night*
> *where the sacrifice of humans is offered as food for the gods*
> *is this what God has prepared us for*
> *to be tried for treason for doing nothing*
> *but bowing to Him and asking forgiveness*
> *for some great sin we know nothing of?*

I stood in the midst of a crowd of people in chains that clanged as they walked and singing a hymn proclaiming they belonged only to Him and awe at the silence of God.

Was this the same God to whom I had given my allegiance? Was this bondage of our own doing, or did God not care?

> *earth, earth, where is your God now?*
> *He that has no ears cannot hear*
> *He that has no heart cannot love*
> *He that has no strength cannot shield*
> *and yet He still calls for us to be on bended knees to Him*

The chained are the Christians, refusing to be persuaded to bow to another God. While over the hill a new enemy began to rise and spit a fire that made our weapons of ultimate destruction obsolete. Their weapons, silent as a still morning, stirred the calm in a moment, sending fire and rain and wind. No one could stop them; no one knew how.

Where would we find rest? The Christians had been swept up by our own intolerant regime, and now a new enemy over the hill was marching towards us.

> *earth earth where is your God now?*
> *the children haven't a chance to dream dreams*
> *the young couples barely have a night together*
> *and for what*
> *— to be torn apart before morning comes*
>
> *our kings have eyes of blind reason*
> *and are seeking to imprison their own citizens*
> *for merely believing in a God*
> *do these Kings see not the enemy on the horizon?*
>
> > *. . . and then there was a terrible light*
> > *. . . and the wind blew more fiercely*
> > *than at any other time in history*
> > *there was not a human alive*
> >
> > *i was transported to an island*
> > *where i saw a man building a shelter*
> > *to shield him from the night*
>
> *come with Me*
> *where there is no book*
> *no church*

no government
no university
only one clean brook
I will never again promise
what I cannot do
and yet you must still
walk out your destiny
for I am the only God who rules

I lay still in my dreams, not wanting to move or stir. I asked myself and anyone who could hear: How many new starts have we? How many seasons and years do we have to make of it what we will?

Of Pearls and Men

"Every grave has a pearl; every pearl bears a sword."
I heard these words in my dream and I remember thinking to myself, what does this mean?

I heard the sounding of guns in the distance, while this voice inside spoke to me over the cacophony," Beware of the new arms, which will break the light into pieces and scatter the particles even into the gates of My throne. War has been in the hearts of man since the beginning. I fear I have failed."

The scene shifted and now I was a frightened child running through the Forest of Fate.

I ran till I fell, out of breath, and when I looked up I was at the foot of a large stone. On it were the words:

"To all who stop here and read this, know it is a new revelation – I am the pearl of great price and now I must fight for it if I am to remain as your God. I ask you to be willing to give up your life for Me, for there is no pearl as great as I. When you are slain I ask only that you lift your arms to Me, and raise not your arms against any man, and I promise I will not make this demand of you again. Nor will I count you guilty again of any crime towards Me. It is I who ask your forgiveness."

Are we now forever not be guilty before you?

Are You fighting in the heavens for You, and how did this happen? Are You saying You have failed in Your creation of us and other creations as well? Are you saying you bear the responsibility for our failure because it is Yours?

Is our death here a victory for You in heaven if we allow ourselves to be martyred?

It Just Was

It was a "wave of motion" that could be sent to any point on the earth, where it would cause an eruption like a severe storm or earthquake. No bombs, no planes, and no way to stop it.

It just was.

This weapon was revealed after a period of time called *"The Great War of Bombs."*

Who could have predicted this? America has surrendered her land to save her people from a weapon so powerful that none could deny it or fight it.

Bread and Butter and a Bomb Are Our Peace

Who are they who built this weapon
    and sent the armies of peace into our land?
We never imagined we would be the invaded ones

Who are the Red men ransacking our homes?
    what means the iron fist sewn on the uniforms?

    bread and butter never looked better
    — my eye is only on the food
    in the distance new york is dying
    — we are conquered and cold.

From across the ocean the slanted eyes decided our fate
How is it we had caused such a hate?
The lesson learned is they who have the might
also decide who has the right

We think they are the evil ones
They think the same of us
We are the same in our suspicion
the difference being — what —
that they have slanted eyes and eat rice
and we prefer bread and butter?

Was a new history being written as I slept and dreamed?

Where Brick and Steel Cringe

where brick and steel cringe
at the shadow of man's revenge
where war and destruction
are a last hope for men who do not understand
that they are imprisoned spirits
captive in their own souls
and war is from within
and the rage of being enslaved
causes such a hate that it seeks to conquer
those who cause the pain

   is there a way out?

where brick and steel cringe
at the hot poisoned wind
where kings and children seek
the same hiding places
revenge held in too long
blames everyone and even itself
for to love or die with this kind of revenge on our hands
is a hate that hates life itself
and purrs for the sin that
allows it to live

   is there a way out?

neighbors steal the bread from anyone who has it
there is no truth sacred enough to keep
man is on the brink of destruction
and we all seek one last meal before the end

where is the glory of a martyr
against a weapon with no noise   no casing   no steel
this weapon touches the hem of heaven
to unleash a wind that sucks in everything in its sight
only to spit it out

is there a way out?

the eagle cannot fly
the dust weighs it down
the earth is blind
there is no way out
but to call out to death
and hope our life is taken

did we die for righteousness or despair?

A New Adam and Eve (1)

1.
a lone man in a small wooden ship
approaches a shoreline

aware of his loneliness
he screams his name to remind himself of himself

but the voice inside only repeats
a new name and a new history

"i am adam. . . . i have died and i have returned
and i live in you."

the voice haunts the man in the small wooden ship
as he sails to a shoreline within his sight

and sees on the beach a woman
who he knows is named eve

eve knows the wooden ship leads her to her destiny
her loneliness lifted when the ship sailed in

the voice inside her convinces her of who she is
her loneliness lifted when the ship sails in

eve's voice soothes adam's loneliness
softly and eagerly she speaks:

> *"i have waited for you a long time*
> *now we will live without shame*
> *you and i are alone on this land*
> *rejoice because we are both here."*

2.

and the voice inside them ministers to them both with these words:

"You will not call upon My name again, for you will have no need. Your life has been purchased and now you are free. The new history of man will have no need to call upon Me. You will multiply on the earth again and prosper, and though good and evil reign in you still, I also reign in you. Look for Me there in the realm where good and evil reign and I will guide you through . . . no other rules, no commandments, no tithes to men or buildings, no loyalty to creeds, no need to pray, for I am with you always.

The earth will remain as earth for a thousand adams are yet to be born, and each adam will live on the earth, and I will give each one a new message with which to serve me."

A New Adam and Eve (2)

I, Adam, sail in a small crudely made wooden ship approaching an unknown land.

I, Adam, the man, steadily rowing my boat, navigates with eyes upon the shore, doing so not for the destination but from desperation.

My heart is heard around the world, and the world waits for me to find a home.

My breathing is hard as I reach out to the shore to tie my ship to a rock.

I am the only ear; I am the only arm; I am the only thought. I am teacher and student, surgeon, inventor, and sole provider.

I am the new Adam, leader of the world. There is no one else to take the role or challenge me.

i am God's nightmare and i am my own nightmare
i will go it alone this time and i will not call upon God
though He may call upon me
i have no more guilt to carry

I am free of the need to know Him. I will follow my dream, which leads me to a woman called Eve. I know this because I know this . . . and the mystery of it will go on forever.

i am adam
son of God
and son of Man
i am and will always be
human.

A New Adam and Eve (3)

Adam lies on the shore, sleeping, turning and tossing to the sound of the sea slapping the rocks in a rhythm that seems to move his sleep into a dream with memories of the past. And then the past forms into a vision of what will come.

As he wakes, the anxiety of the day weighs heavily upon him, and as he contemplates this dream an idea arises in his thoughts about how to navigate to the distant land he could see with this eyes but never seemed to reach by boat.

Where did this idea come from? Adam surmised that it was through God and that this is how God speaks . . . through dreams.

So Adam sets sail for this distant land he can see, to the land where Eve is waiting.

A New Adam and Eve (4)

I saw myself lying on the asphalt street, steam everywhere. A man stood over me and spoke these words: *"Do not search the doorway of God after war. There are no more passages open."*

I arose slowly and looked upon the city, darkness all around. There were no more great lights, no more noises of the metropolis. Then a lonely wind began to sweep, carrying with it a fine dust-like ash. The man who stood over me spoke again, *"Leave no tracks. Walk only when the wind dies and rest when the wind moves."*

I saw an atlas open before me and my own country sending hate eastward half across the globe. Now the west wind was blowing from our back, and with it the ash of our own making. And with the ash came the Maker of Graves — the ash the dirt for the grave; the rubble of the city our gravestone . . . and our souls the carrier of the hate we send around the globe.

The man speaks again, *"May the stench be such a great memory that all the generations after you will fear it."*

I slept for a while and then the man said, *"Do not build here again. This means do not build temples to Me or worship Me; I desire it not. The temples of stone are a witness that its truth has failed. Do not build a building to Me again."*

As I woke I heard: *"There are weapons yet to be built, with no ash and no sound.*

"I must go now and be busy for the earth's breath is almost done. . . . But I have more need of the earth, and so a new Adam will come."

A New Adam and Eve (5)

Adam carefully wrote in his journal as it seemed to him that man should record his journey. "The day is for man; he is not to call upon God nor wait for—or upon—God. The evening is for rest and sleep is the time God calls upon man, through visions and dreams.

"Make no promises to God and expect no promises from God. We are responsible for ourselves. Be not surprised when all goes awry, and when all goes right, rejoice, but rejoice not as if God had performed it.

"Depend not upon dreams and visions every night, or even at all. We cannot make a dream or vision from God appear. If one does appear, and if it happens as it says, then it is God, and if it doesn't, then it doesn't. Care not, for there are no promises that say God has to send you dreams or visions.

"Know that all the prayers and wanting and needing move not the hand of God . . . and that *that* is the mystery of God and man. Above all, know there is God and God is to be feared.

"We waited upon God before and we imagined promises God made to us. We believed we could trust God and then War Three came and destroyed it all. So fear God for what God can do but does not. . . ."

A New Adam and Eve (6)
Dream Series

1. Beyond the doorway

Be still and look inside
I will show you a doorway
Where no spirit has yet gone
Where man has paid the price for his soul
and the messiah guided man in "the way of the sacrifice"

Look what it brought
Look out at the sky
See the last of the earthly lights disappearing
No more explosions or noise
only darkness and quiet
over the whole earth
while the winds blow the ashes of the dead

The guilt of man
that which I laid upon him
was a burden too great to bear
I gave birth to a hate and an evil
I had not imagined possible
Now this evil that has captured man's soul
has to be cast out
for if it is not it will destroy even its own
in order to cause Me to fall

So I created many sacrifices for man
on which to lean till I could rid evil from this realm
And so it was that man had comfort for his soul
though he still struggled with evil

Like a snake that hid
almost impossible to find
man rested
willing to believe a sacrifice
could rid him of his sin

2. *My crime*

But time has failed to make man clean
so now it is time for Me to confess
that I have failed
not man

Now you know that I — God — can fail
and to know that is the greatest trust of all
I give it to you in trust
for mercy is the redemption of my failure
I asked you to give your life away
to make sure evil would have no home
and would roam and be empty of its power
without your soul as its house
Therefore I give you this trust of knowledge
of My own failing
So you can now forgive Me
and yourself

Beyond the doorway —
the new heaven and earth will not burden man
with the guilt of My errors
From now on each man will know God in his heart
and the need of prayer will have no meaning
for there will be no sin
and man will fellowship with God again
in the cool of the eve

Every man will fellowship the same
without fail
This is the new testament I make with
the new Adam

You may enter now.

Last Testament

I require you not to create an altar to me
I make you not guilty of sin

Though in your heart good and evil are of equal strength
and you shall choose one over the other

Though one shall master you
I am with you to choose the good
and if you fail
I will judge you not

> *With no guilt attached the new world starts now*

It has not been fair to burden you with guilt
and allow other men's enslavement of you in My name

I decree that you are not to be subordinate
to any man regarding Me
and that every individual shall have the freedom
to seek Me in his own heart

> *And that no one shall have the right to condemn this freedom.*

Utopia Bazaar

Weaving through the open bazaar, staying under the tents in hopes of shade to provide some relief from the heat, we only felt the hot sun add to the intensity. As we roamed the narrow and crowded paths, I wished for the wind to come to offer a cooling breeze.

The bazaar had every conceivable gift for sale at every conceivable price, from food items, to stones, to cloth, to animals — all was for sale. In my mind I imagined these items to be like our beliefs in God, that we could purchase almost any kind of belief for a price. Purchase any belief you want with the guarantee that it is the best one and it will serve you well.

It was the music that made me stop and listen . . . dancers and musicians, intoxicating to listen and watch, as if the intoxicating feeling was God.

Many joined in the dance and moved to the music, which seemed it could go on forever. Yet soon the sense of evil joined the intoxication . . . like an addiction.

The promises and signs over the entrances of the bazaar tents read: *"Utopia Bazaar — where all things are bought and sold."*

There were materials and tools outside the bazaar area where it seemed anyone could make the same items if they were so inclined to make the effort . . . but it was so much easier to simply buy what one needed than make it oneself.

On the other hand, those who were selling made sure the prices were quite high, in their booths, under the tents of the Utopia Bazaar.

About the Author

Tony Prewit was born in Stamford, Texas in 1954 and then moved with his family at the age of eight to Silver City, New Mexico. He has earned both bachelor's and master's of arts degrees and has traveled extensively throughout the United States as a musician. Besides his interest in poetry, the author has written, directed, and performed in several plays and as a mime actor. In addition, he is an artist who delves in photography, charcoals, pastels, and watercolors. Art is his private therapy.

For over thirty-five years the author kept a journal of poetry that chronicled his most secret, inner struggles with his belief in God. During that time he lived what seemed to be a fairly normal life—traveling, going to school, marrying, and owning a retail furniture company. This journal, however, does not chronicle his "normal" life, but his struggles with belief. He believes many people have these same kinds of inner challenges with life, and this journal brings to the forefront the reality of these challenges.

Since 1978 he has lived with his wife Pat, a classical pianist, in Silver City, New Mexico, the place he considers home for its culture, land, seasons, and people.

www.ingramcontent.com/pod-product-compliance
Lightning Source LLC
Chambersburg PA
CBHW052111090426
42741CB00009B/1759